A Country Christmas

A color Therapy Coloring Book

By

Kim Jordan Blair

I would like to thank my dear friend Mary Ann Morrongiello Manders for coloring the picture on the cover of this book.

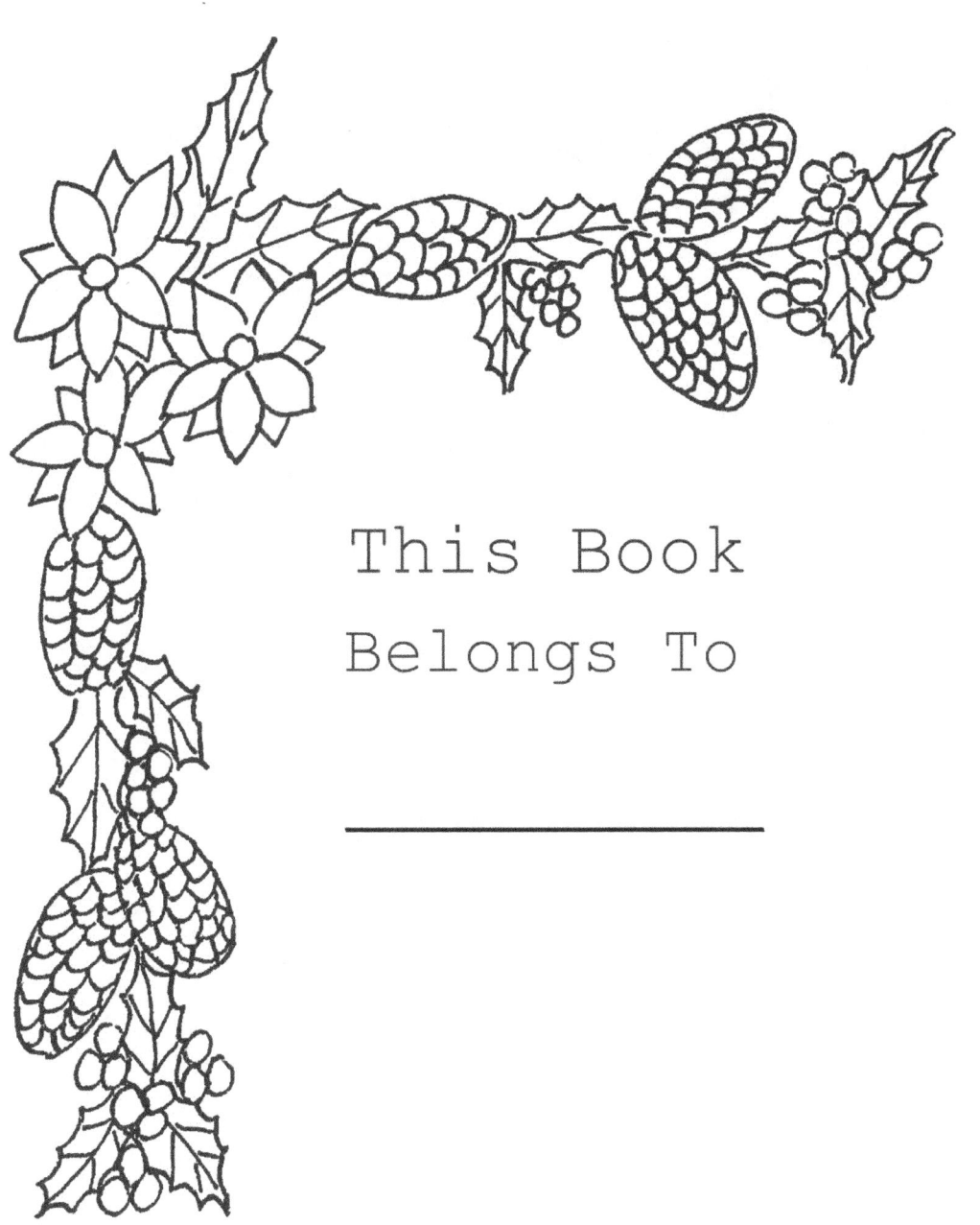

This Book
Belongs To

_____

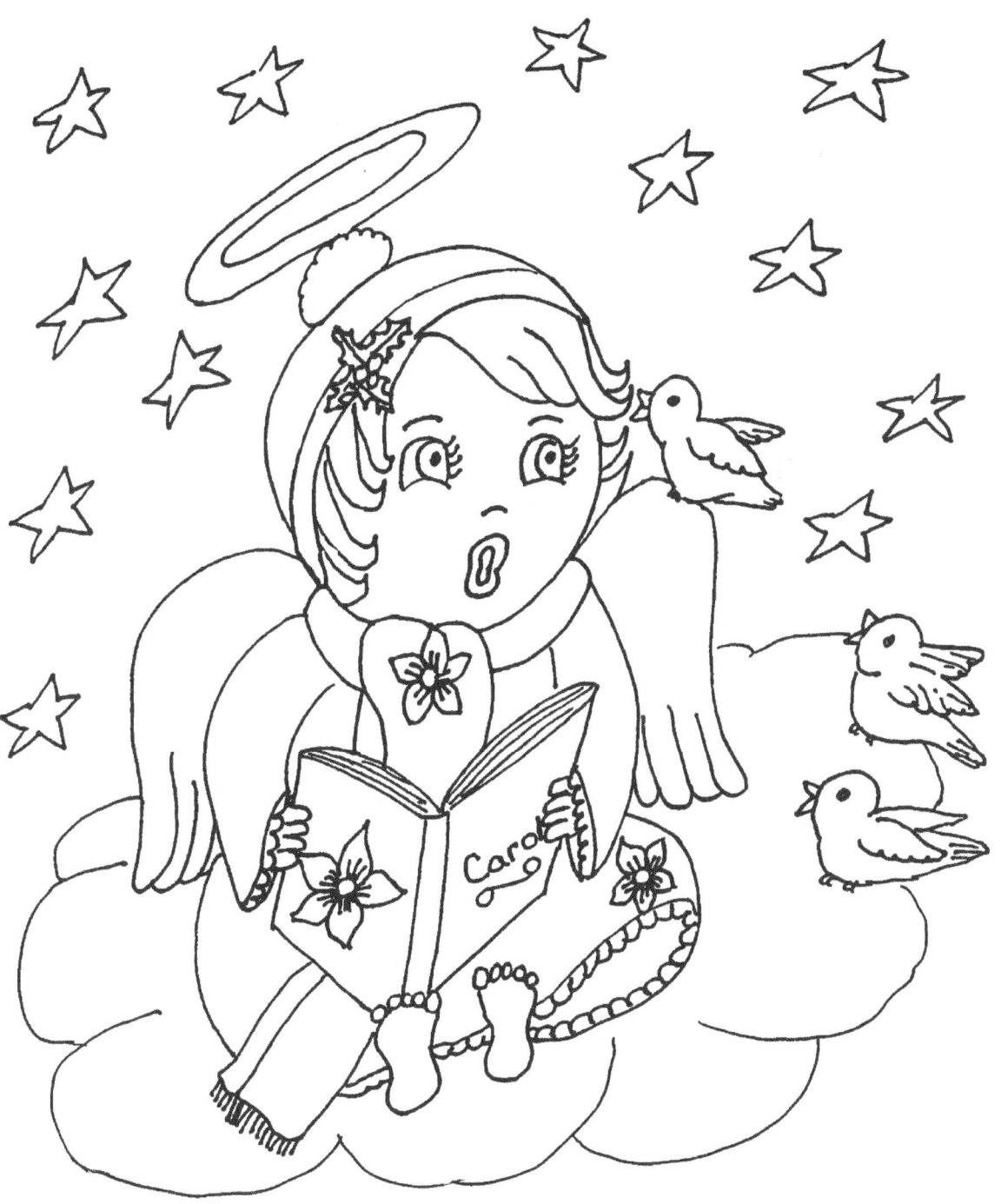

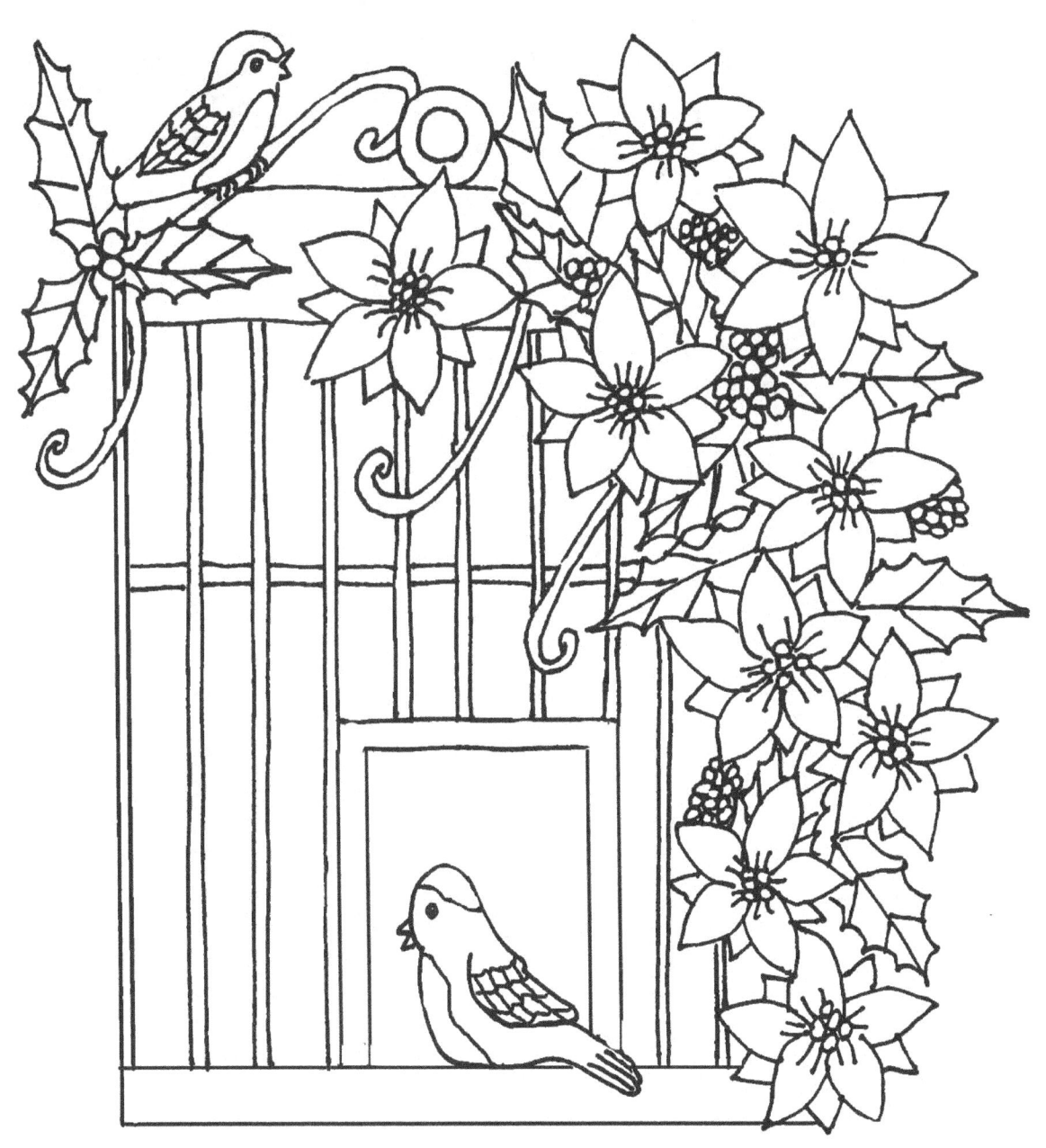

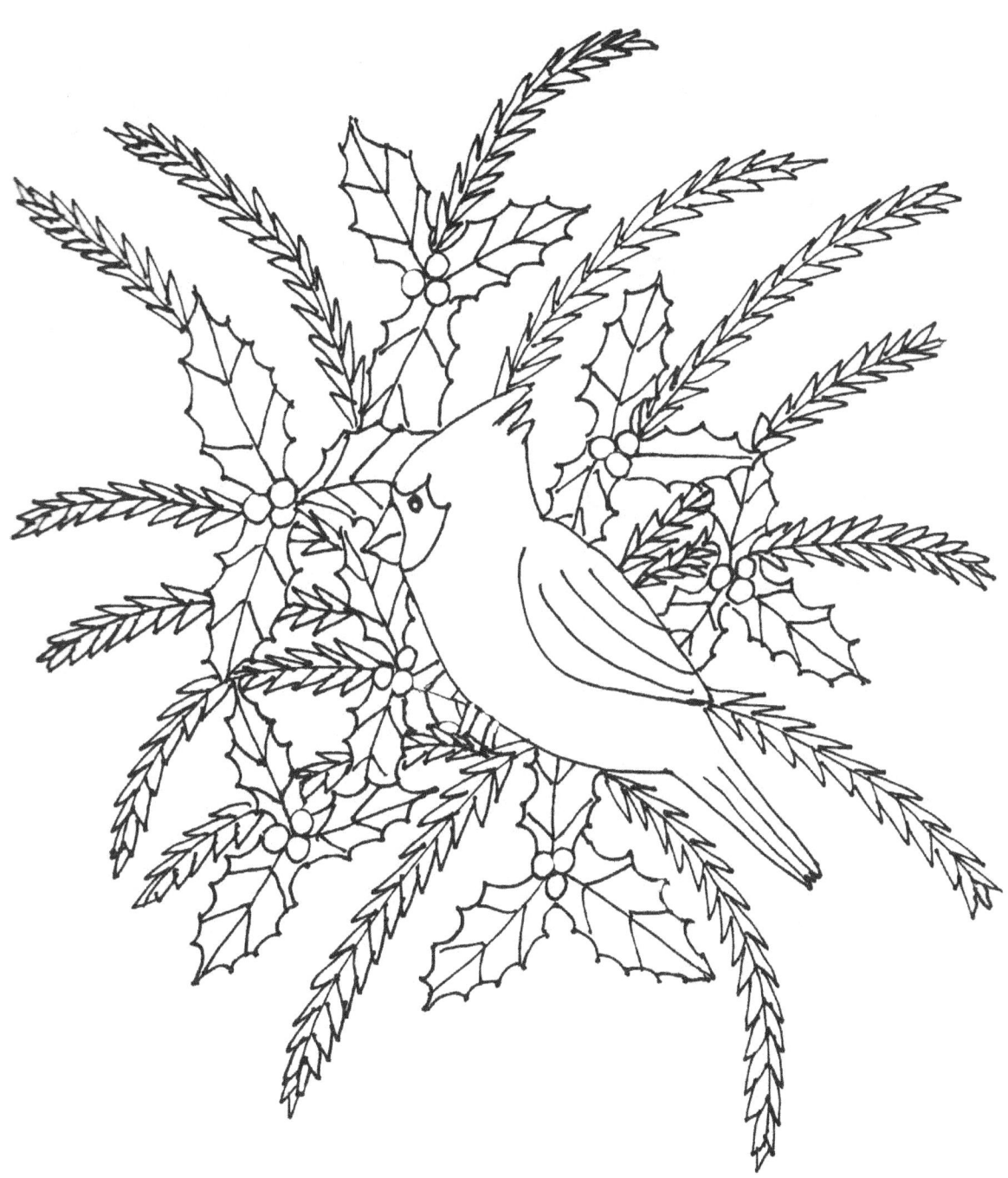

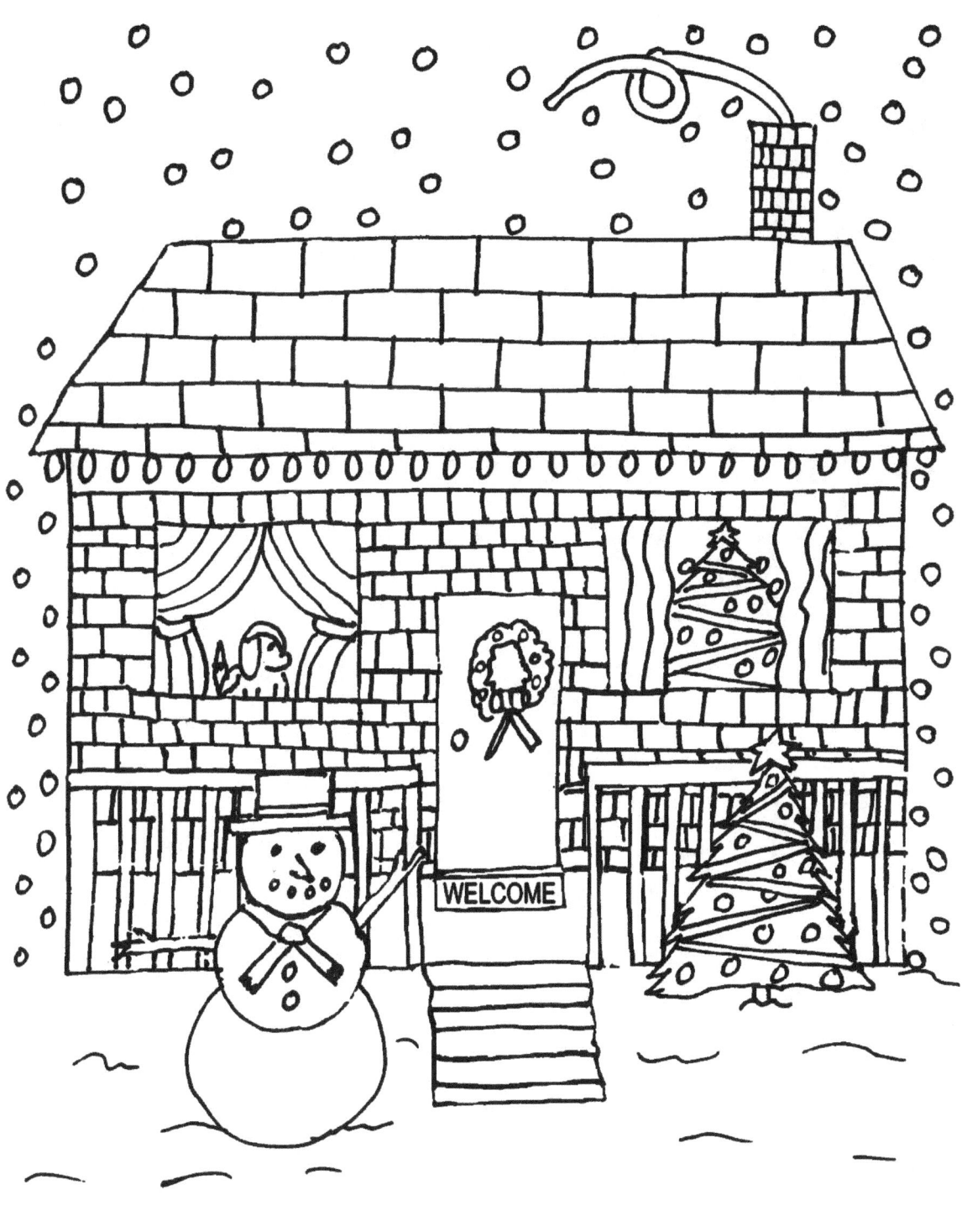

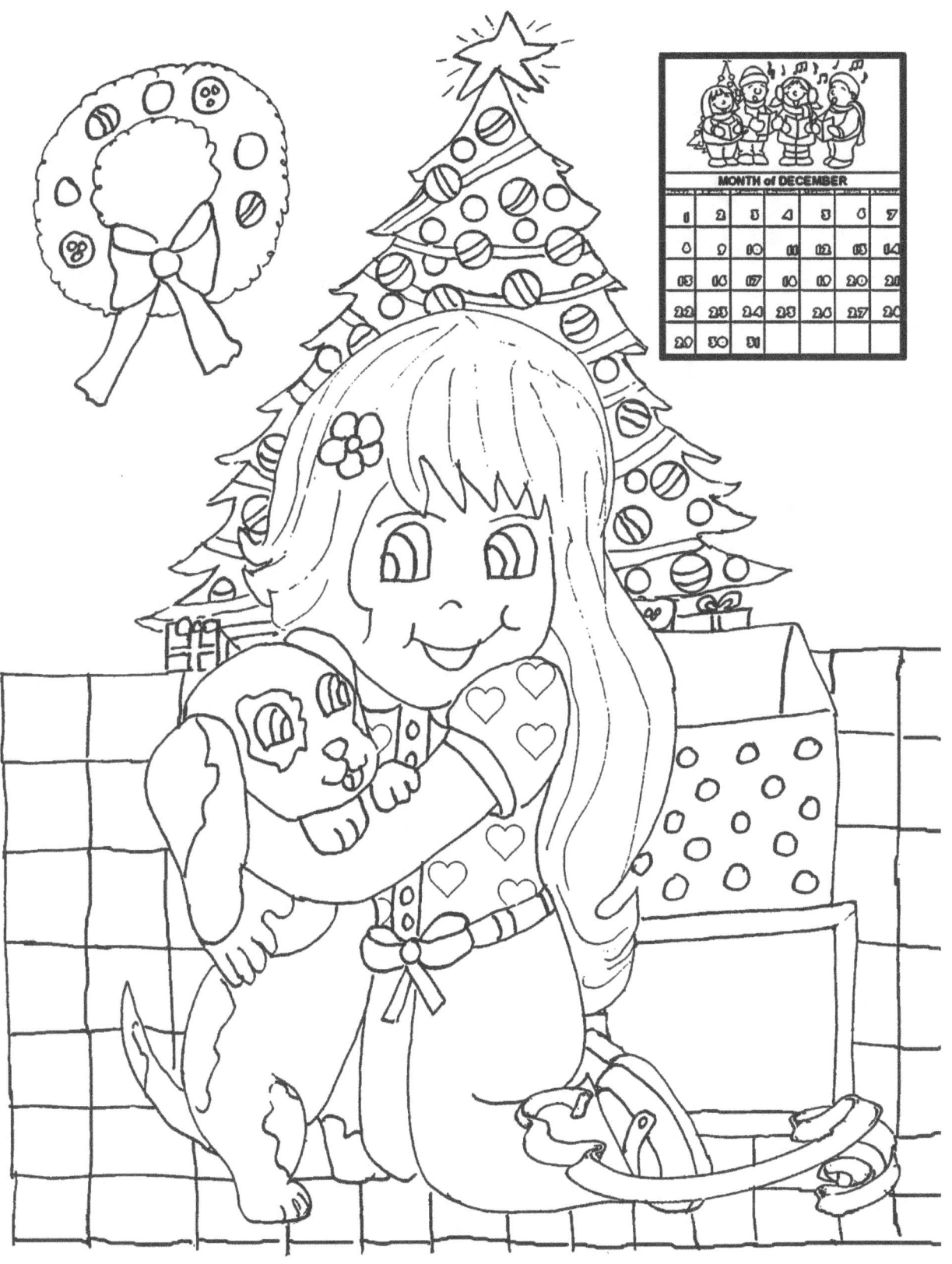

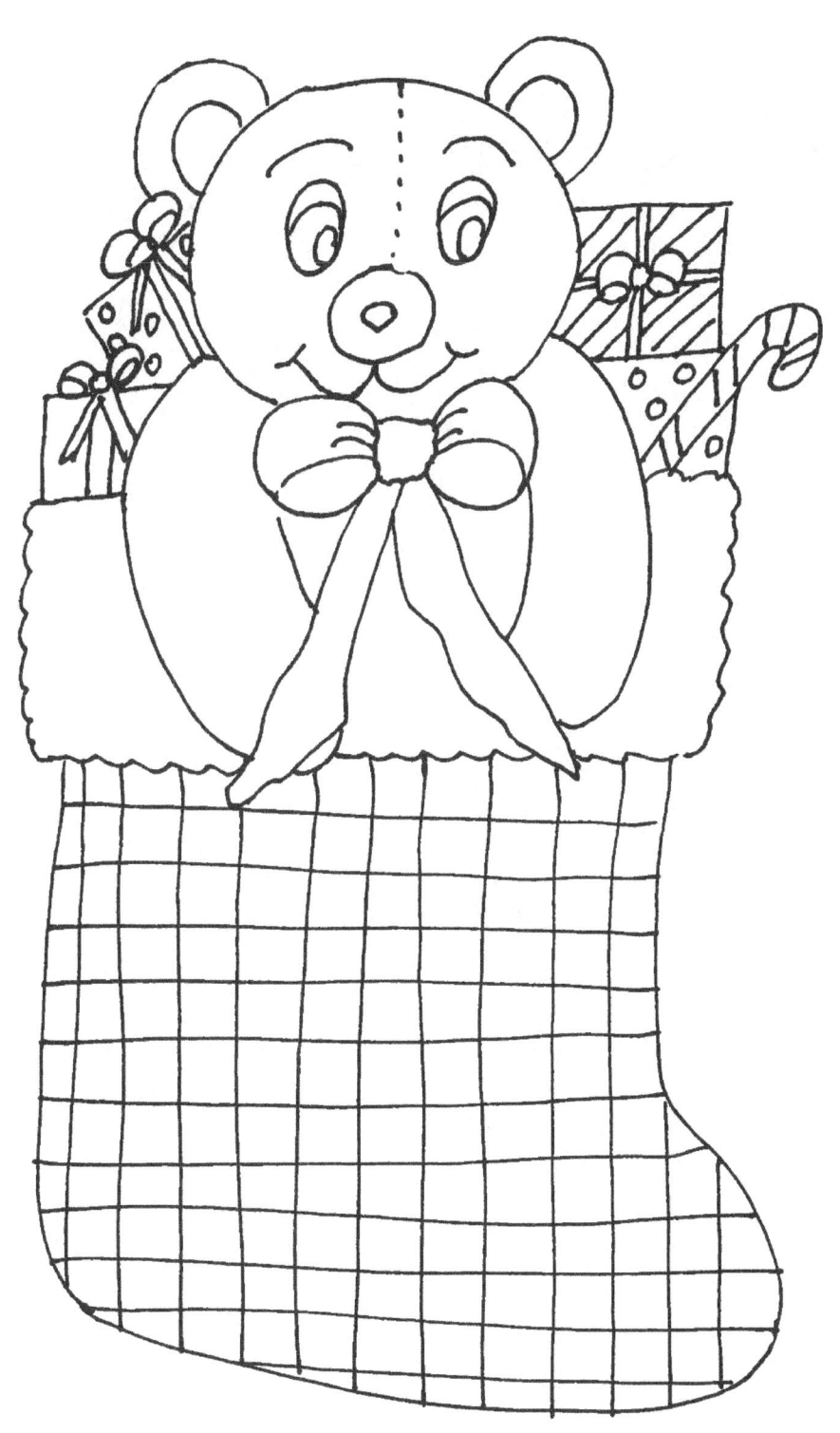

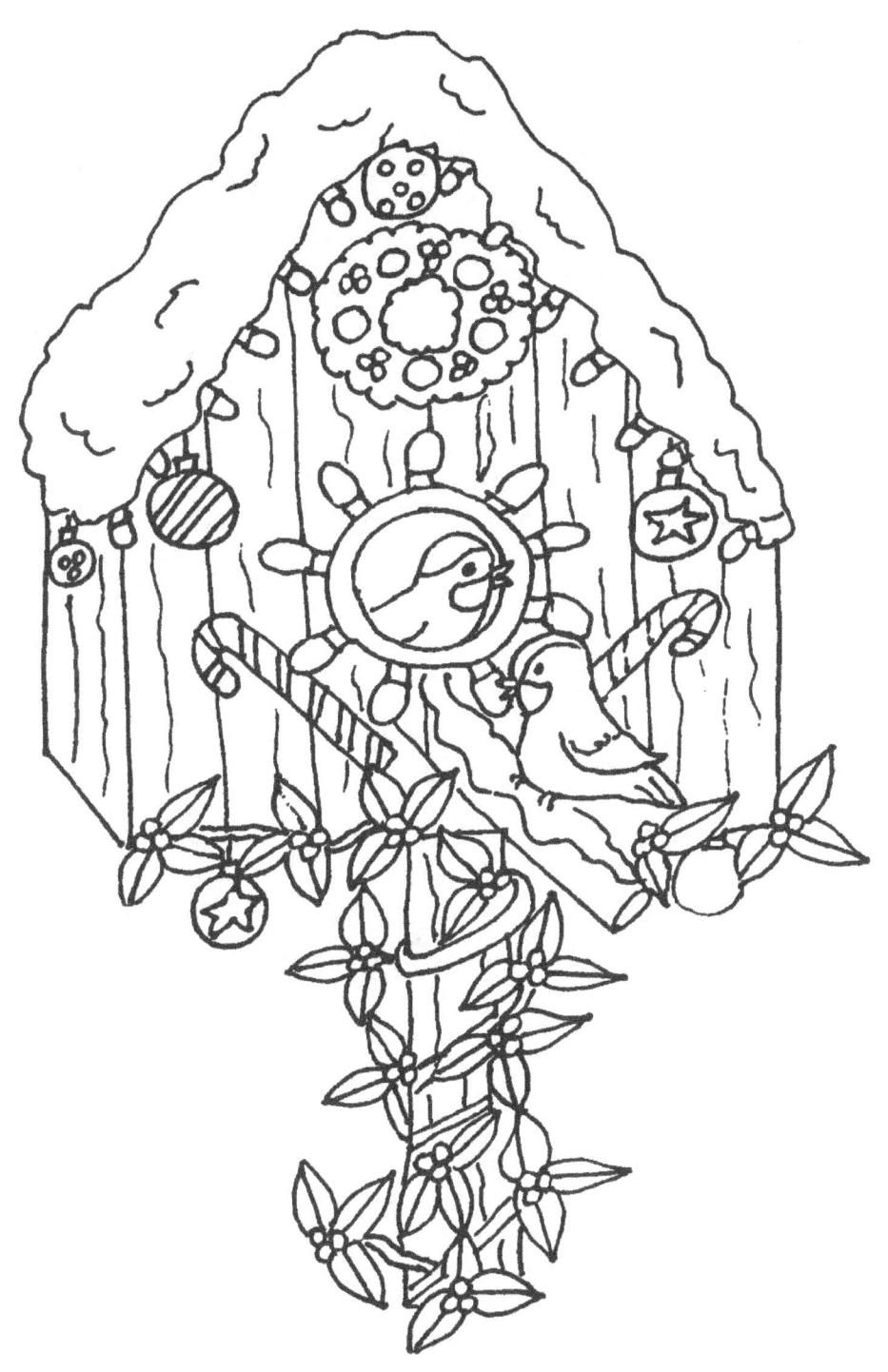

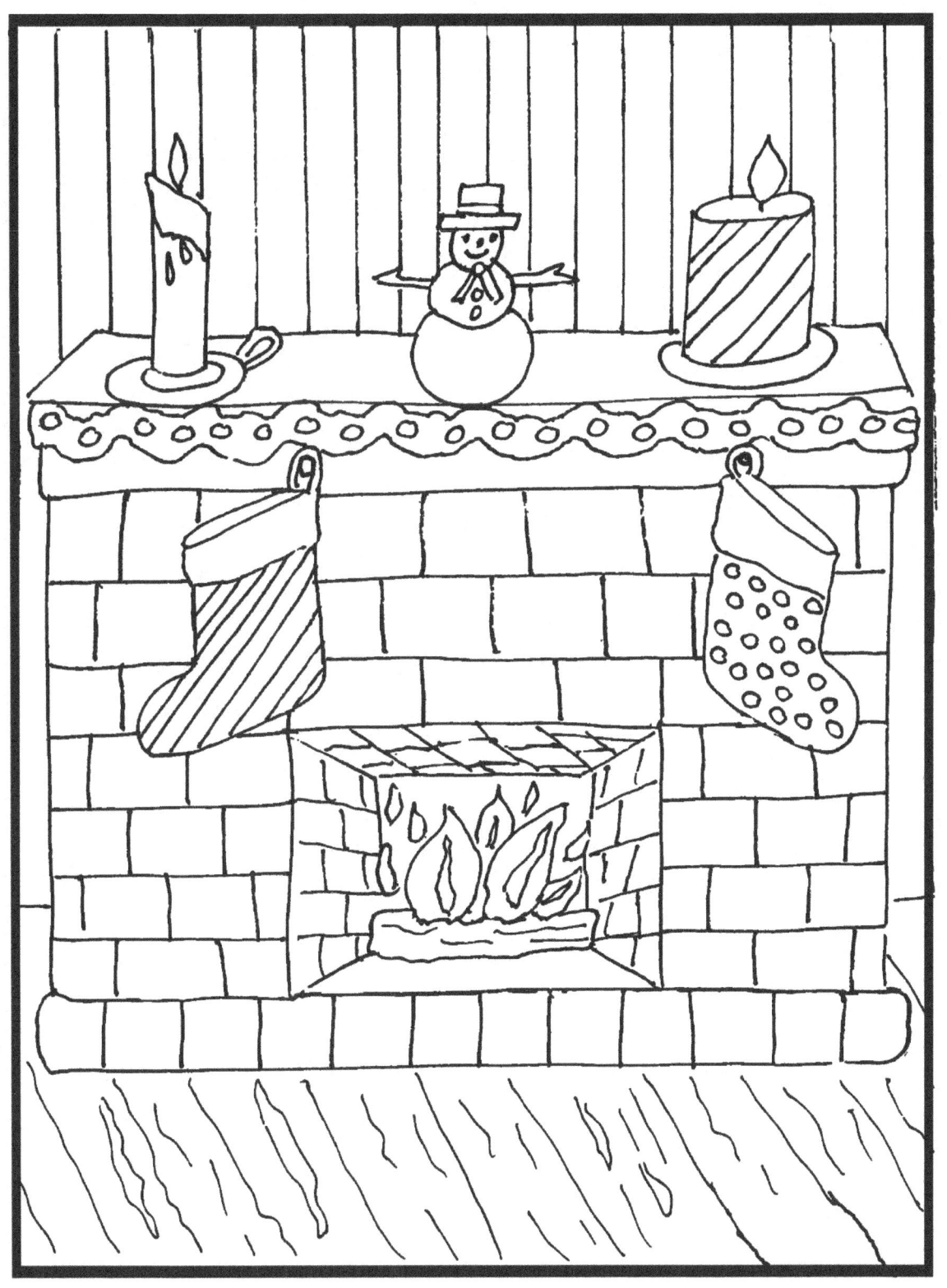

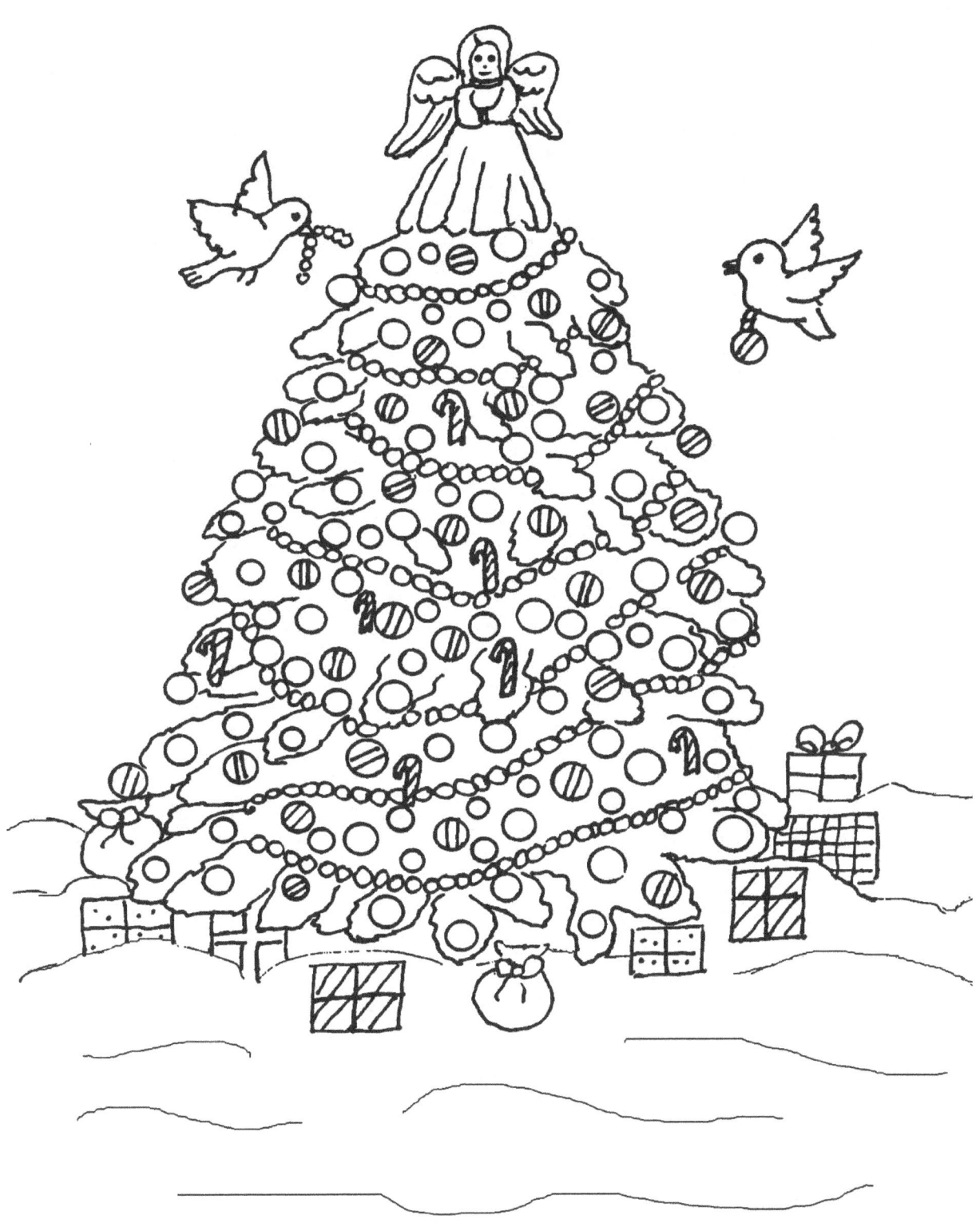

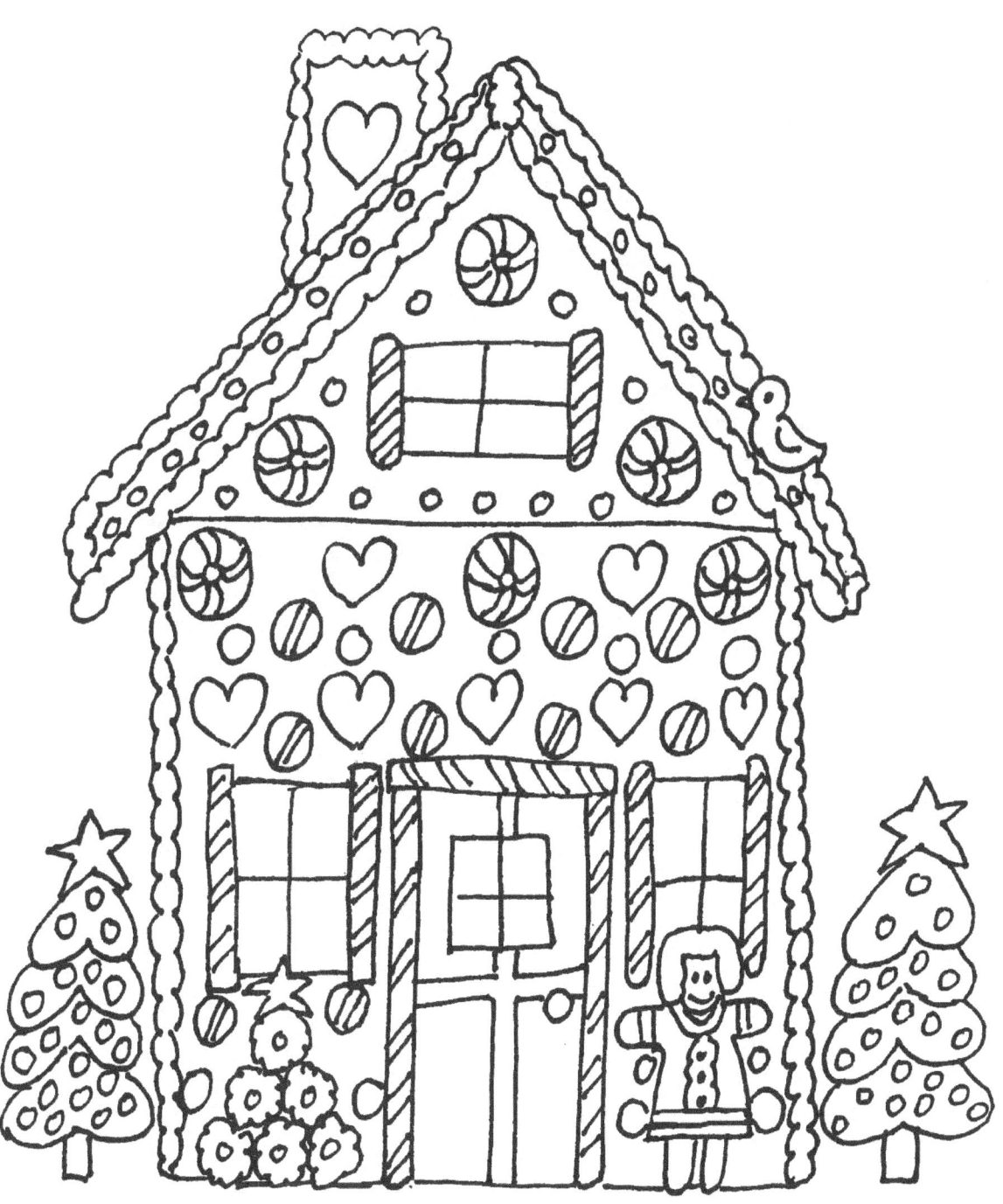

Fear not; for behold I bring you good tidings of great joy which shall be to all people

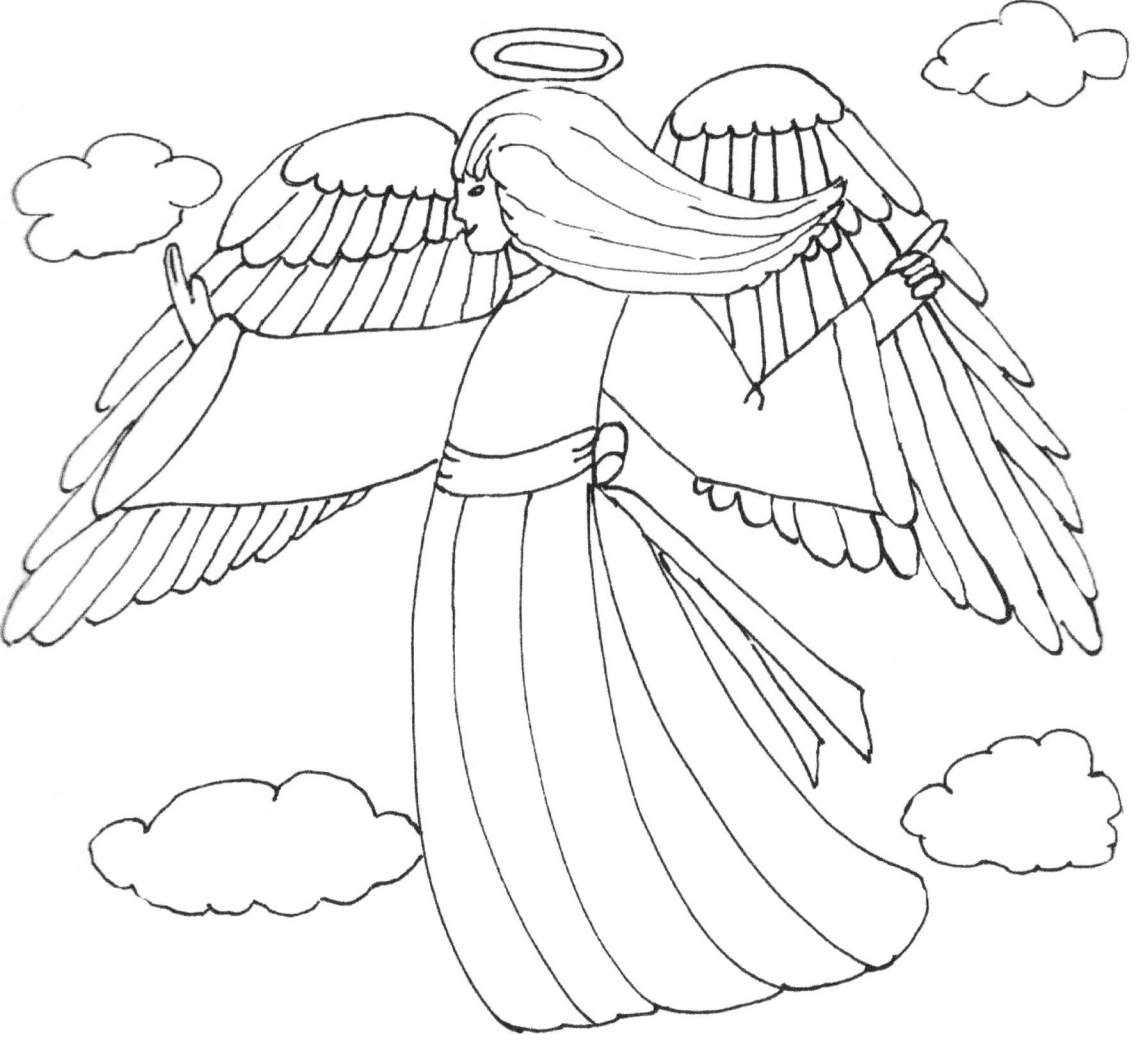

For unto you is born this day in the city of David a Savior which is Christ the Lord

Luke 2:10-11

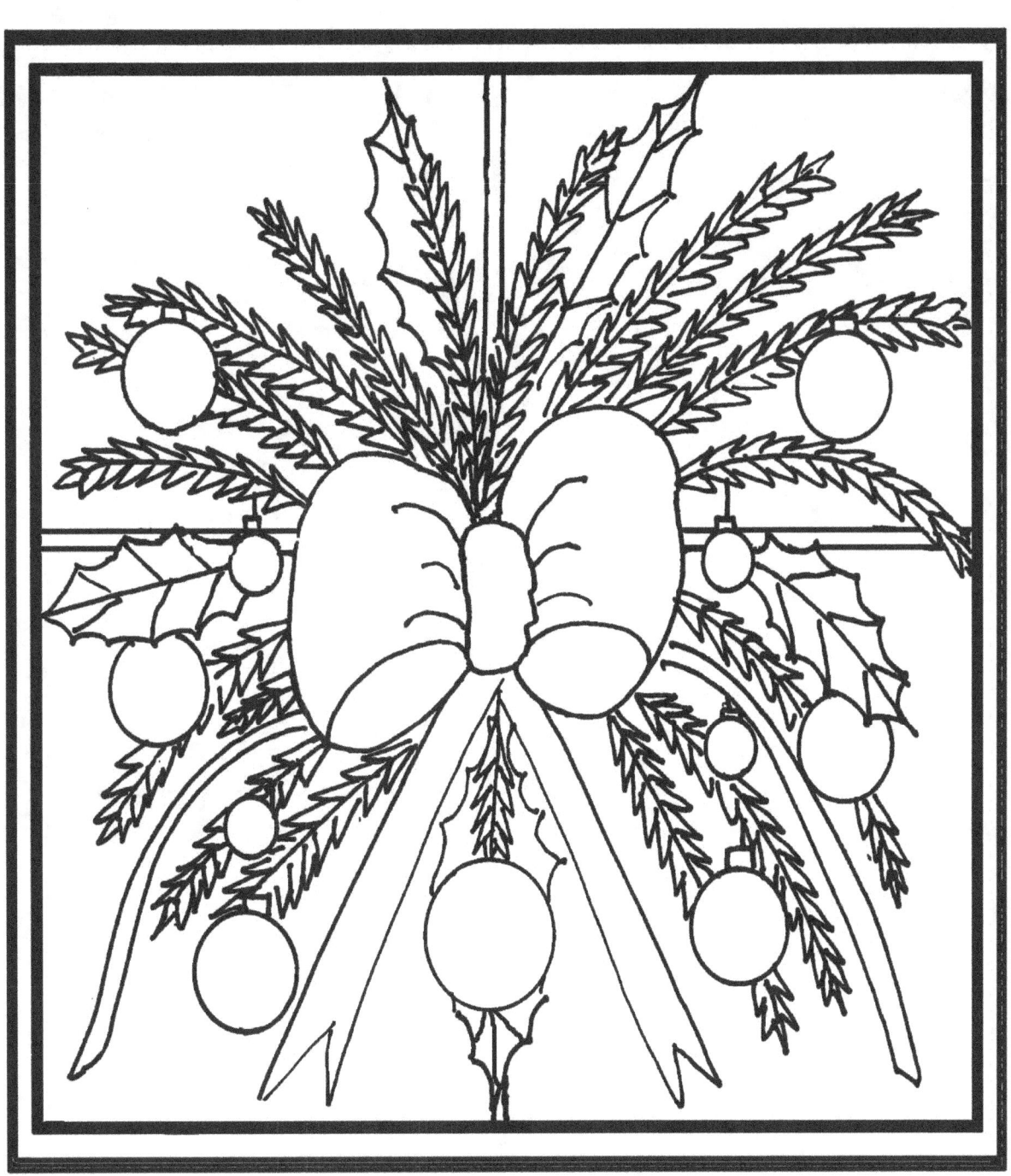

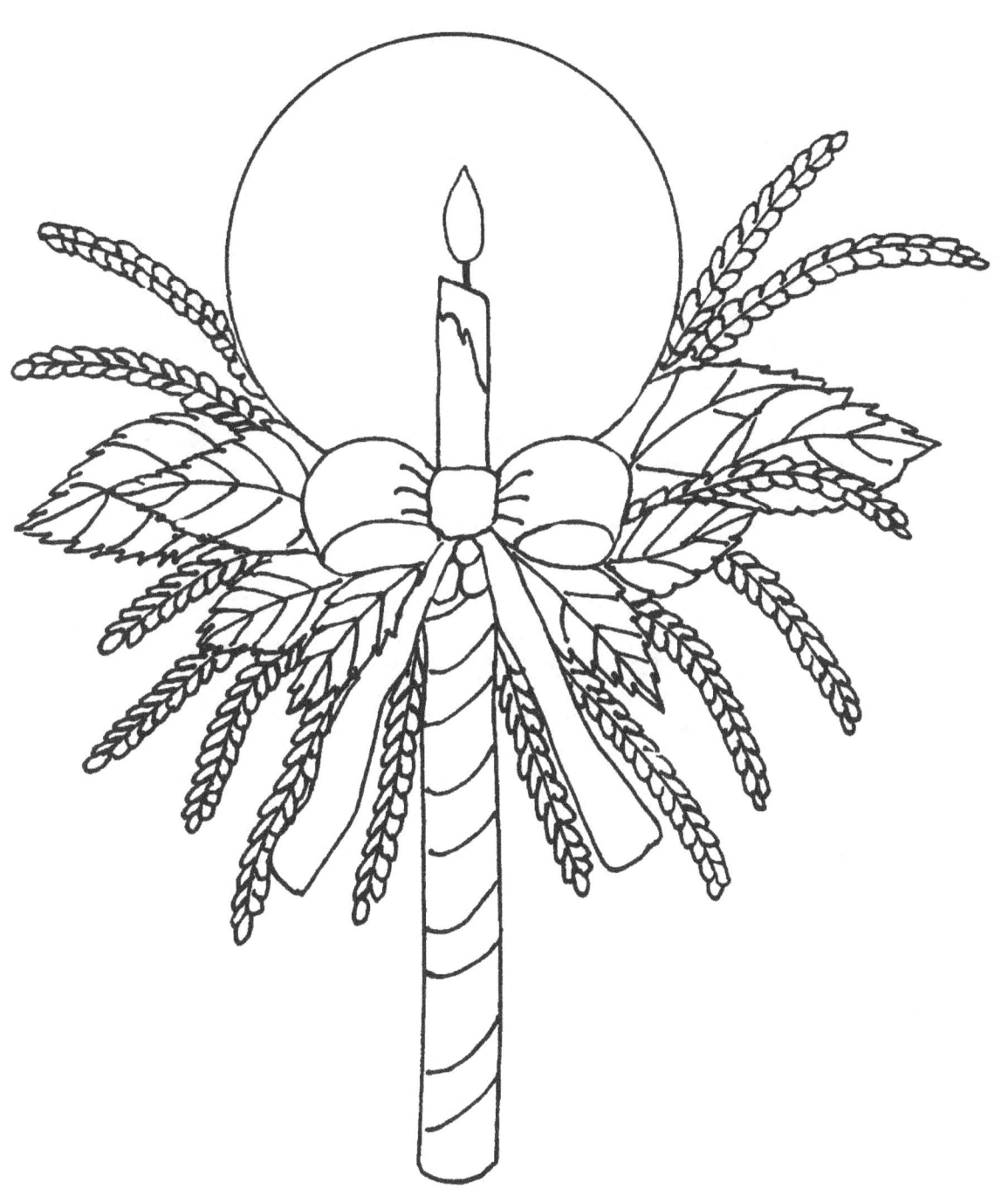

Not A Creature Was Stirring

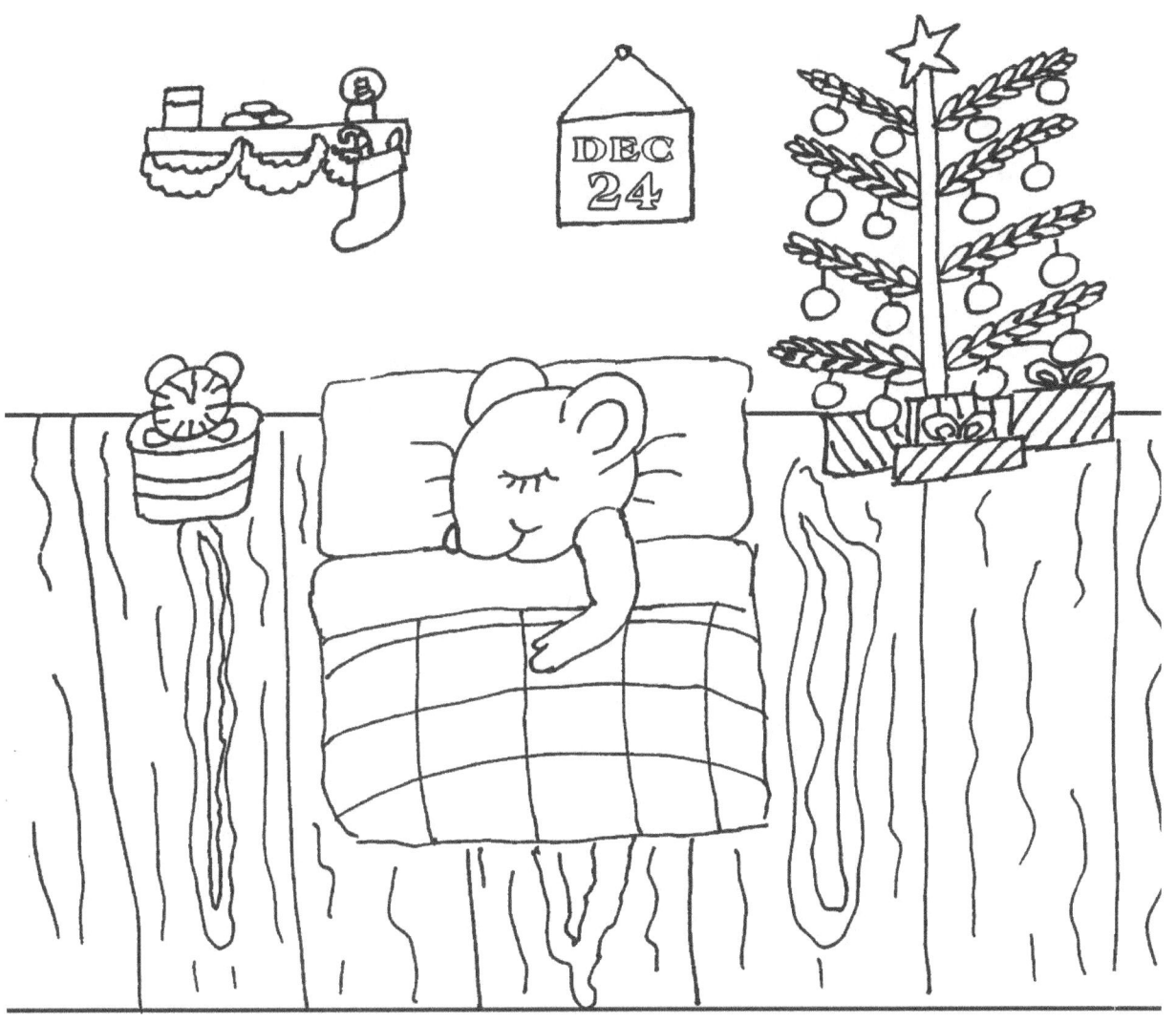

Not even a mouse

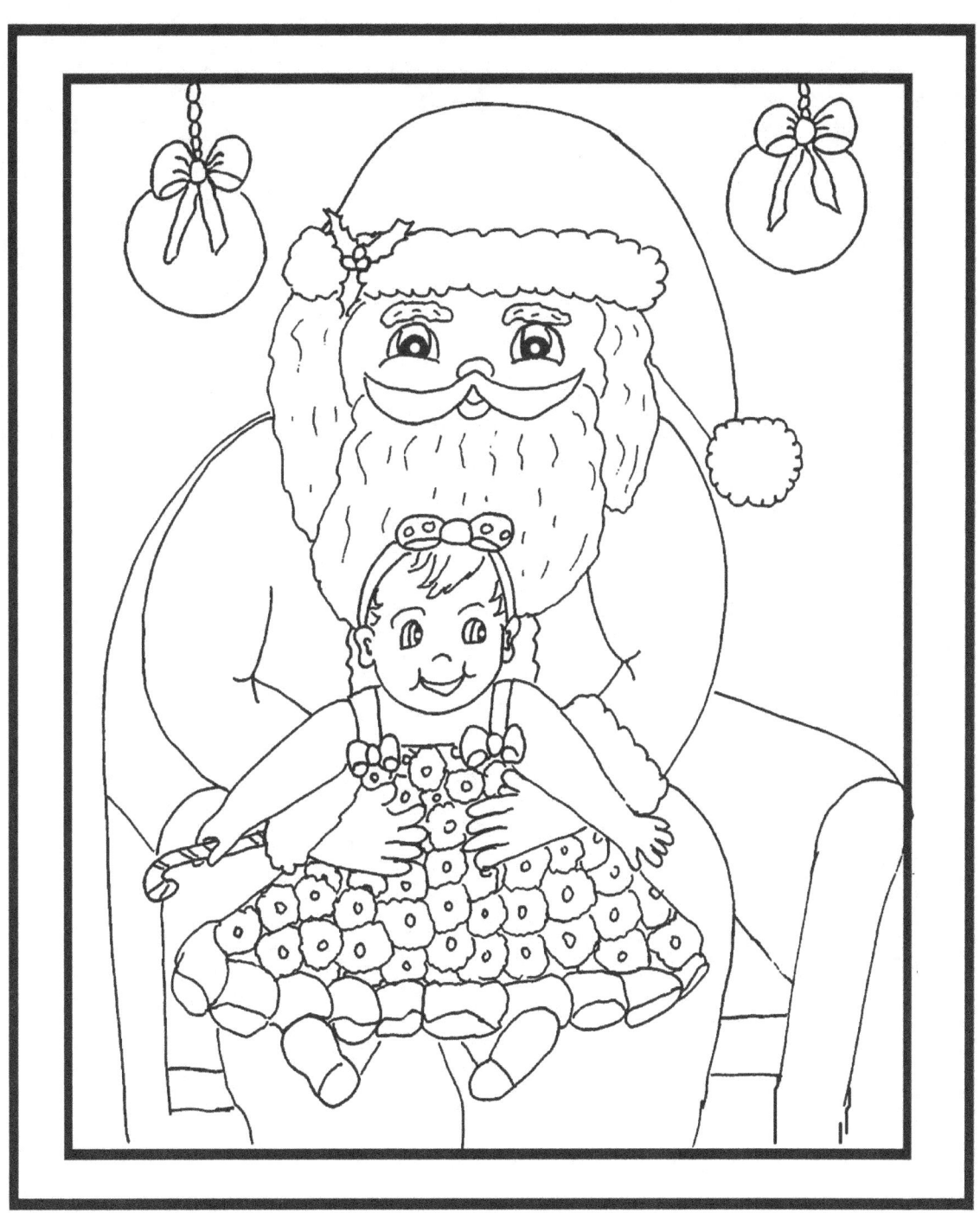

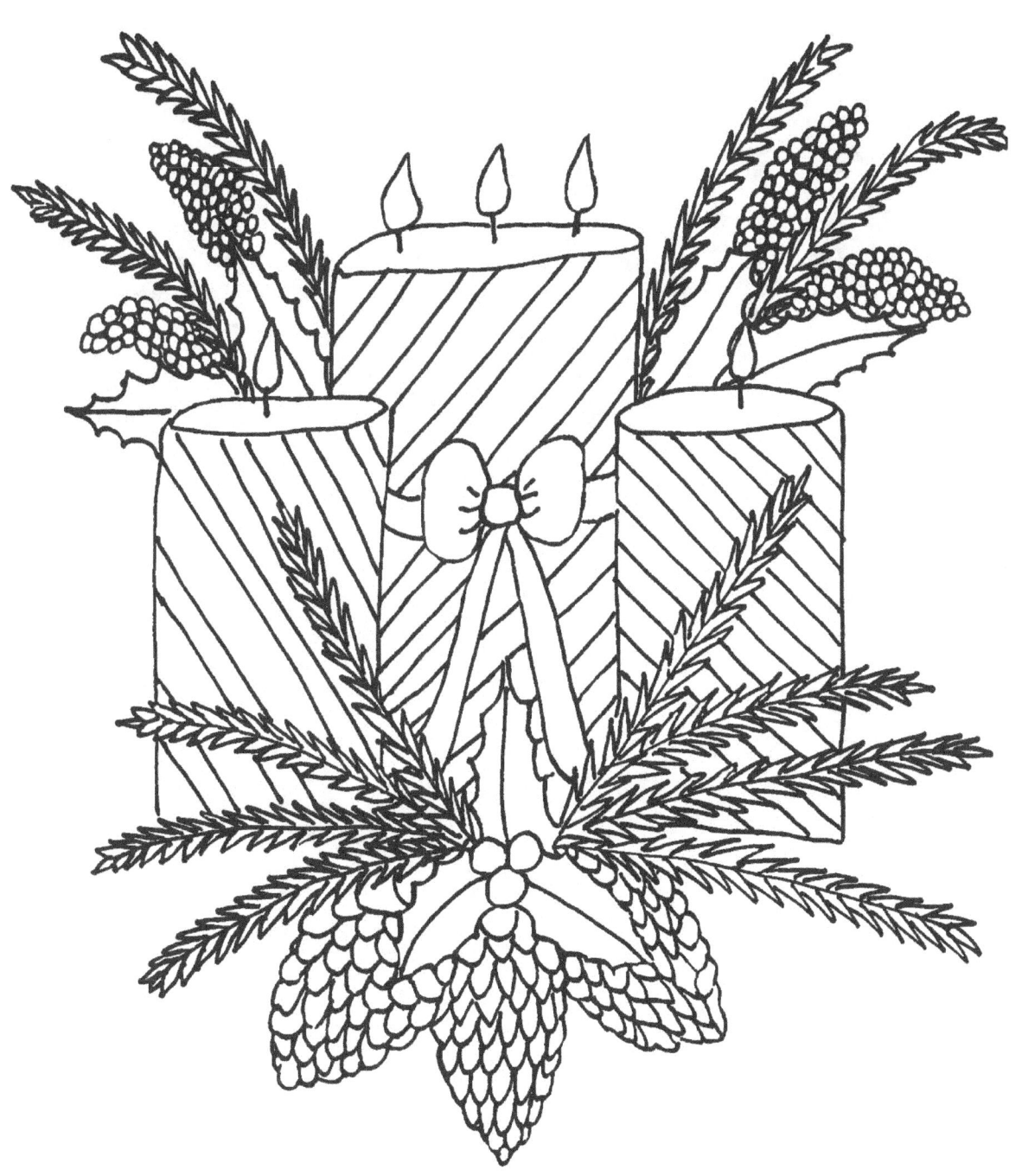

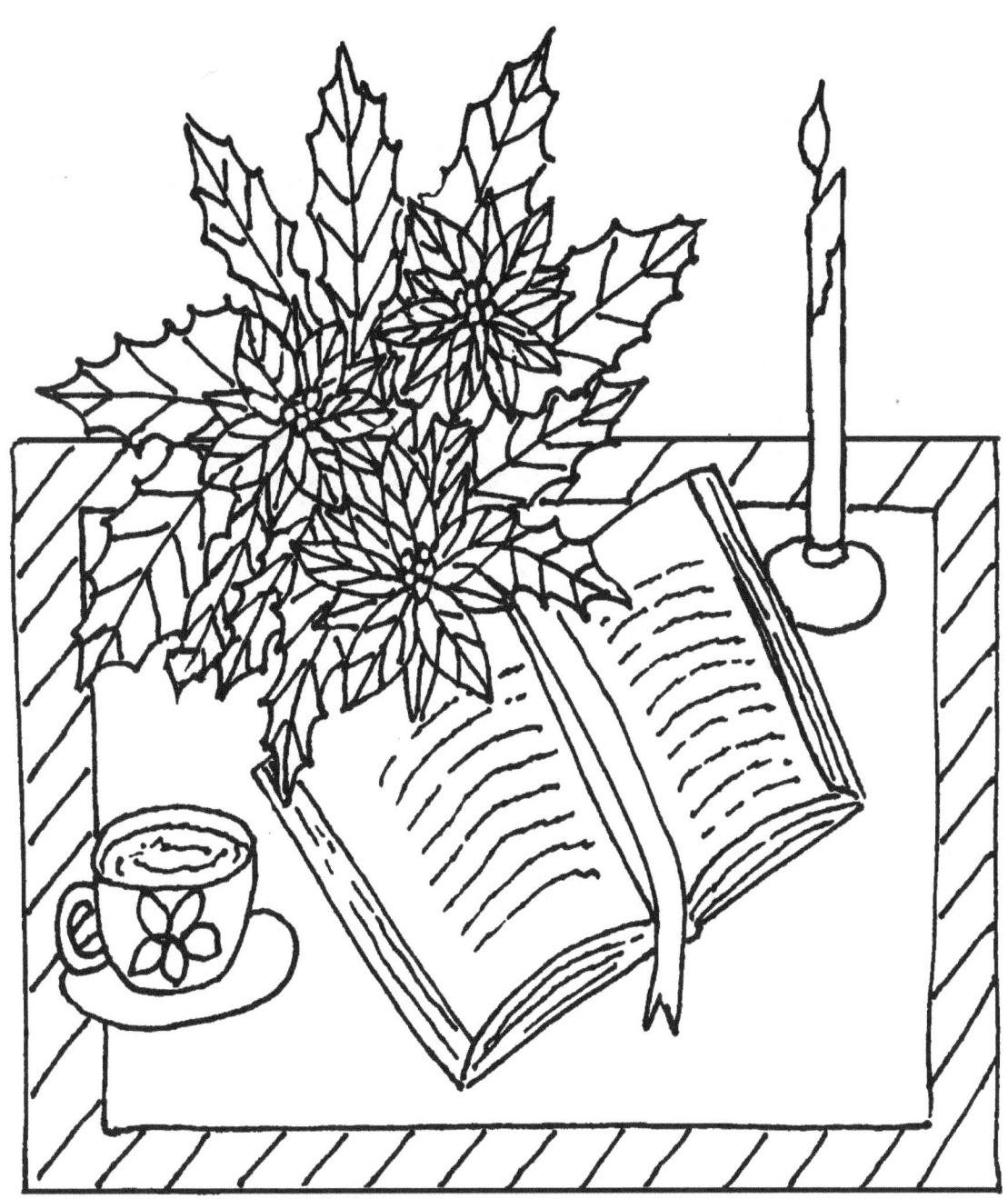

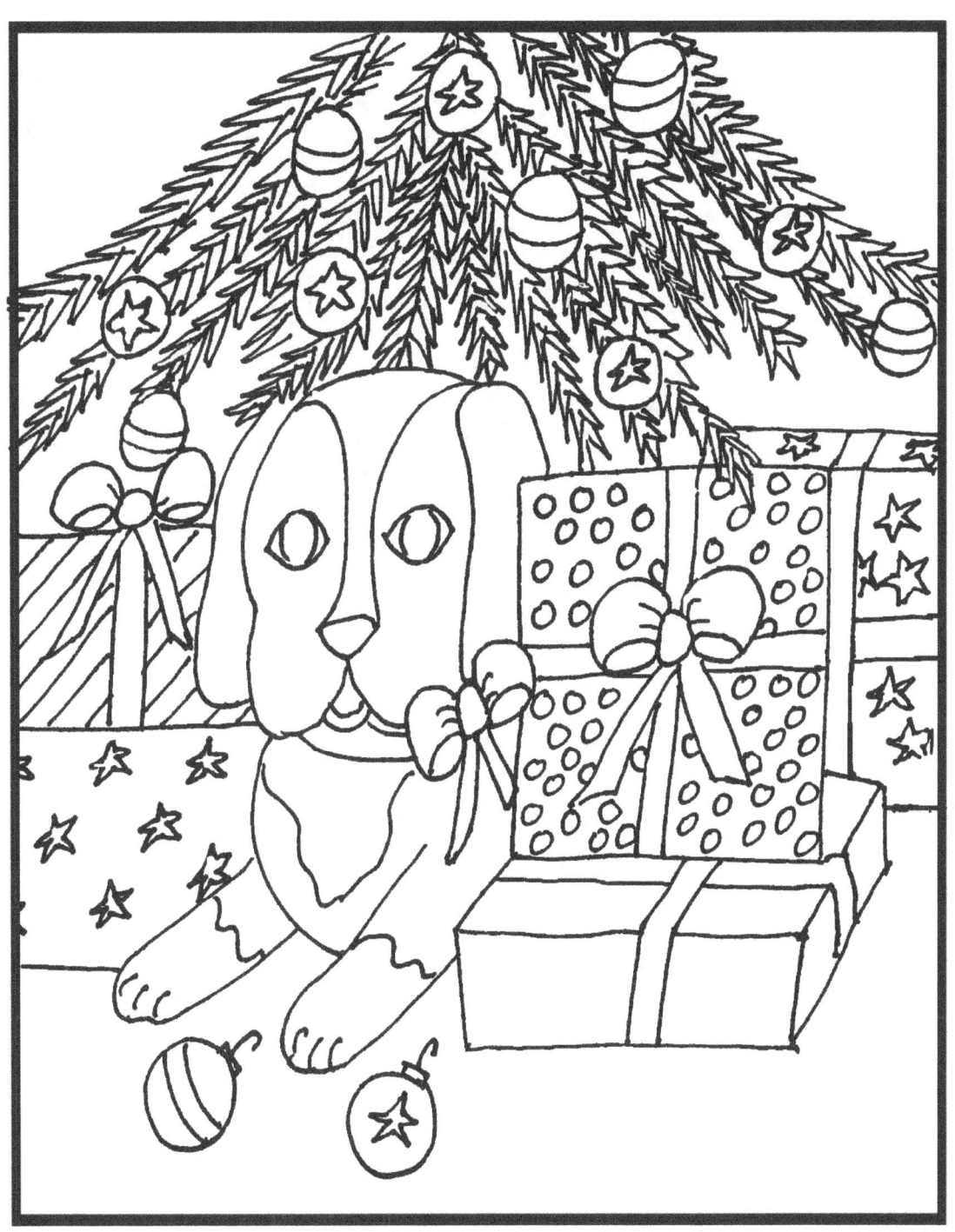

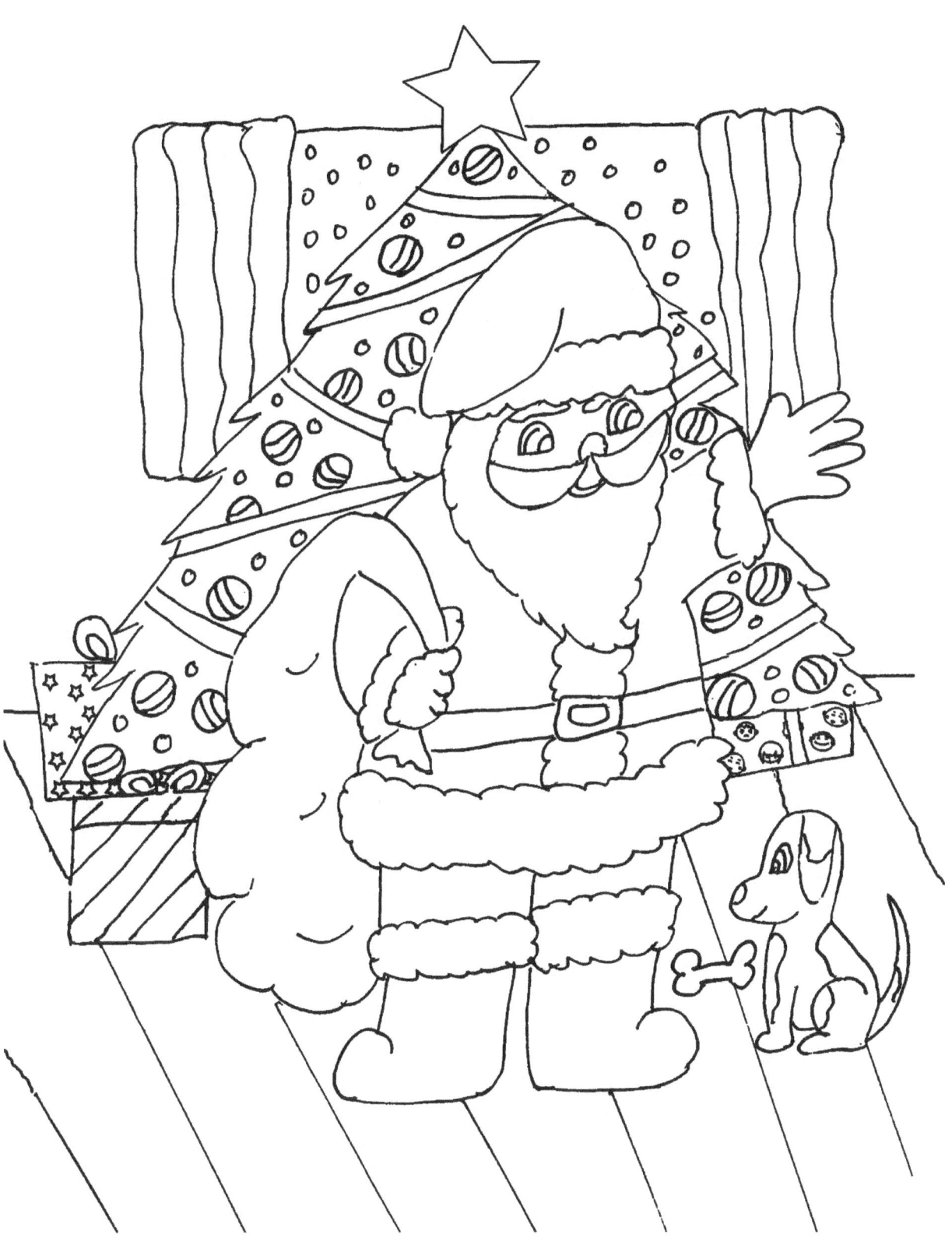

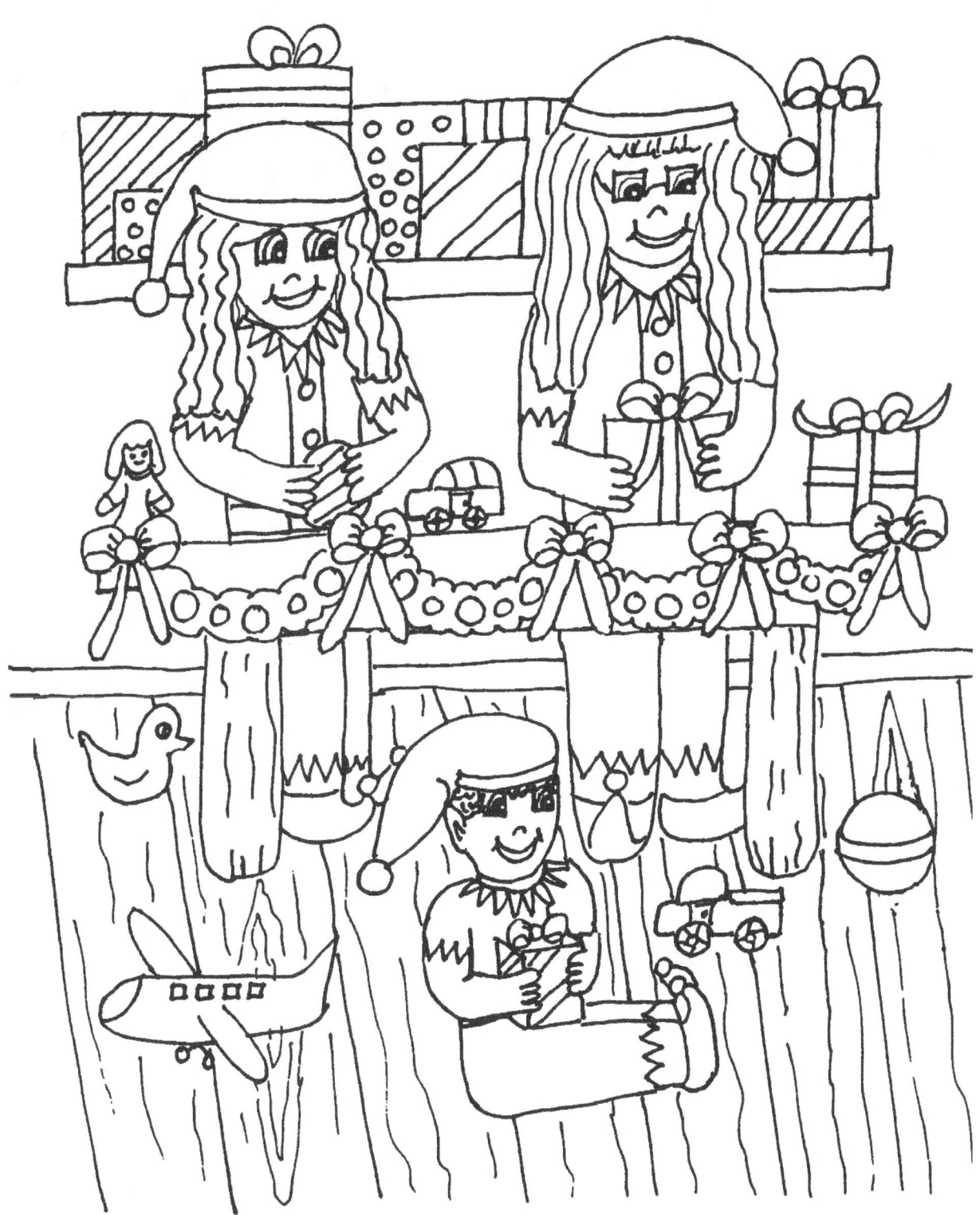

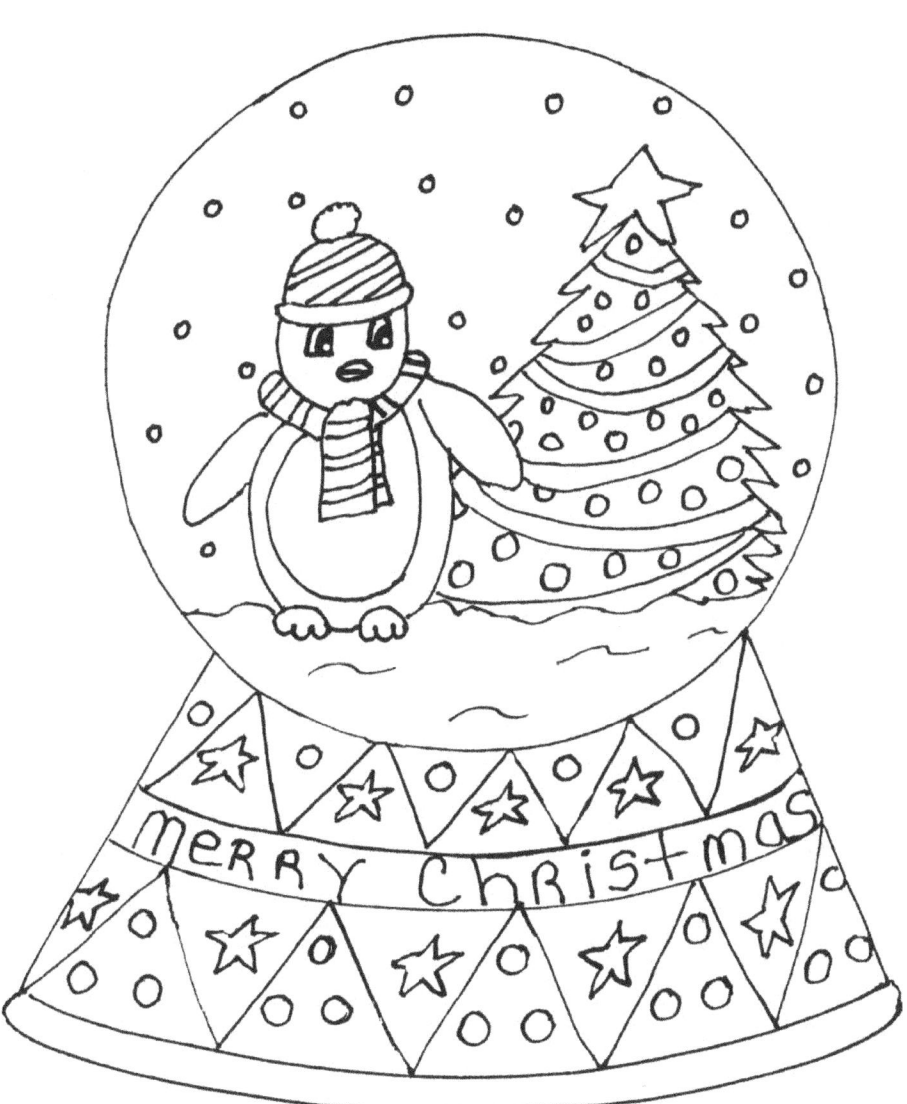

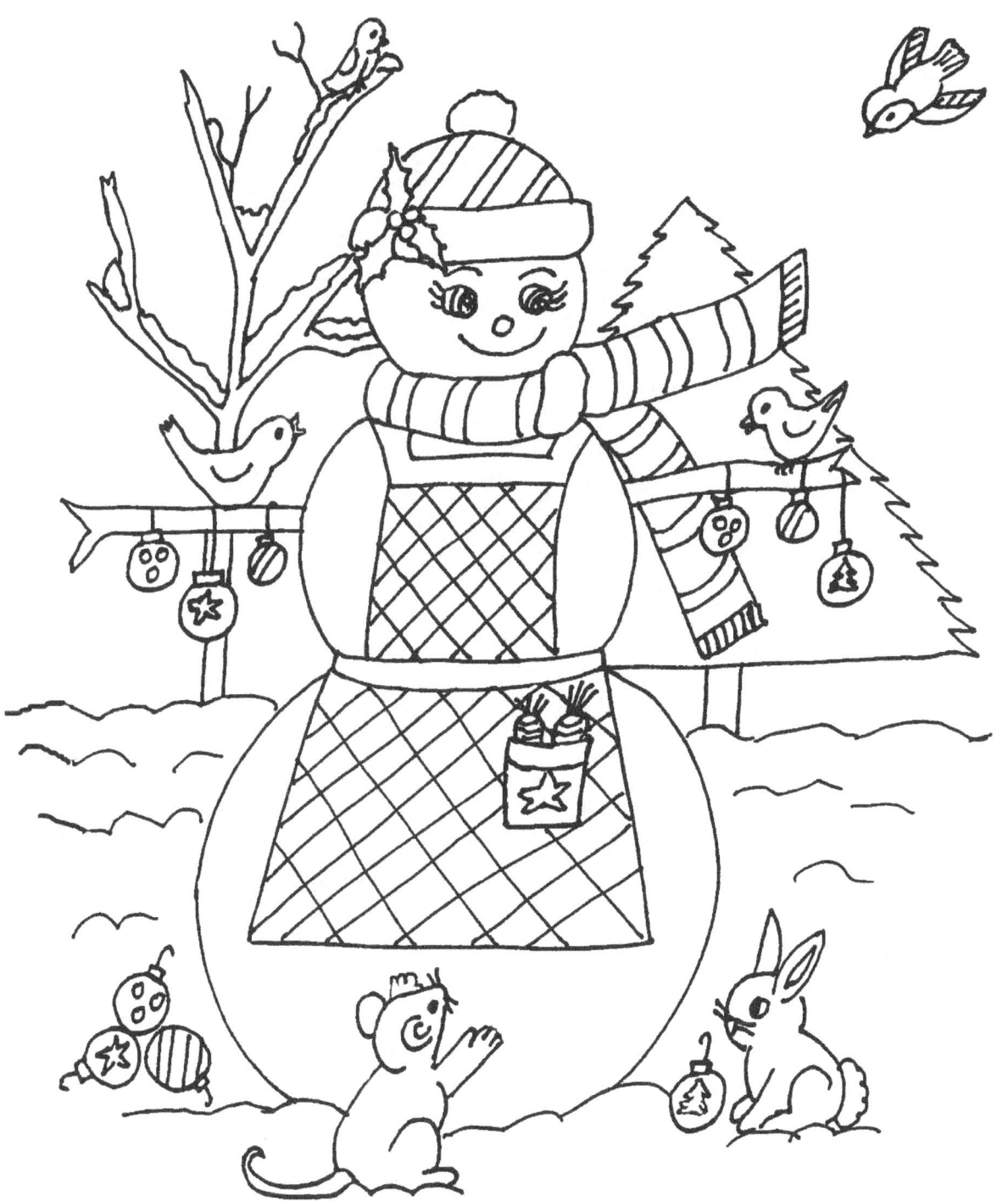

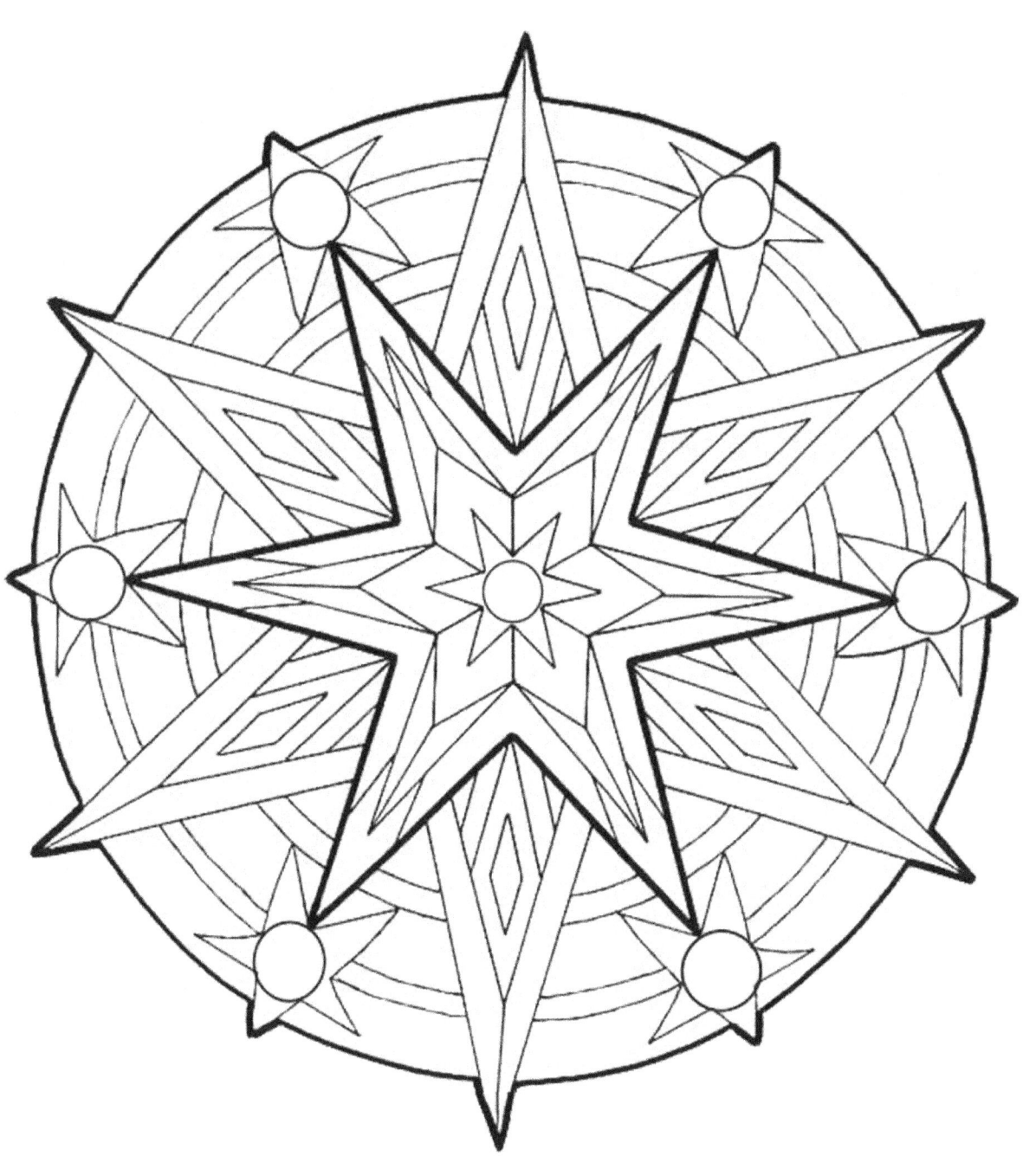

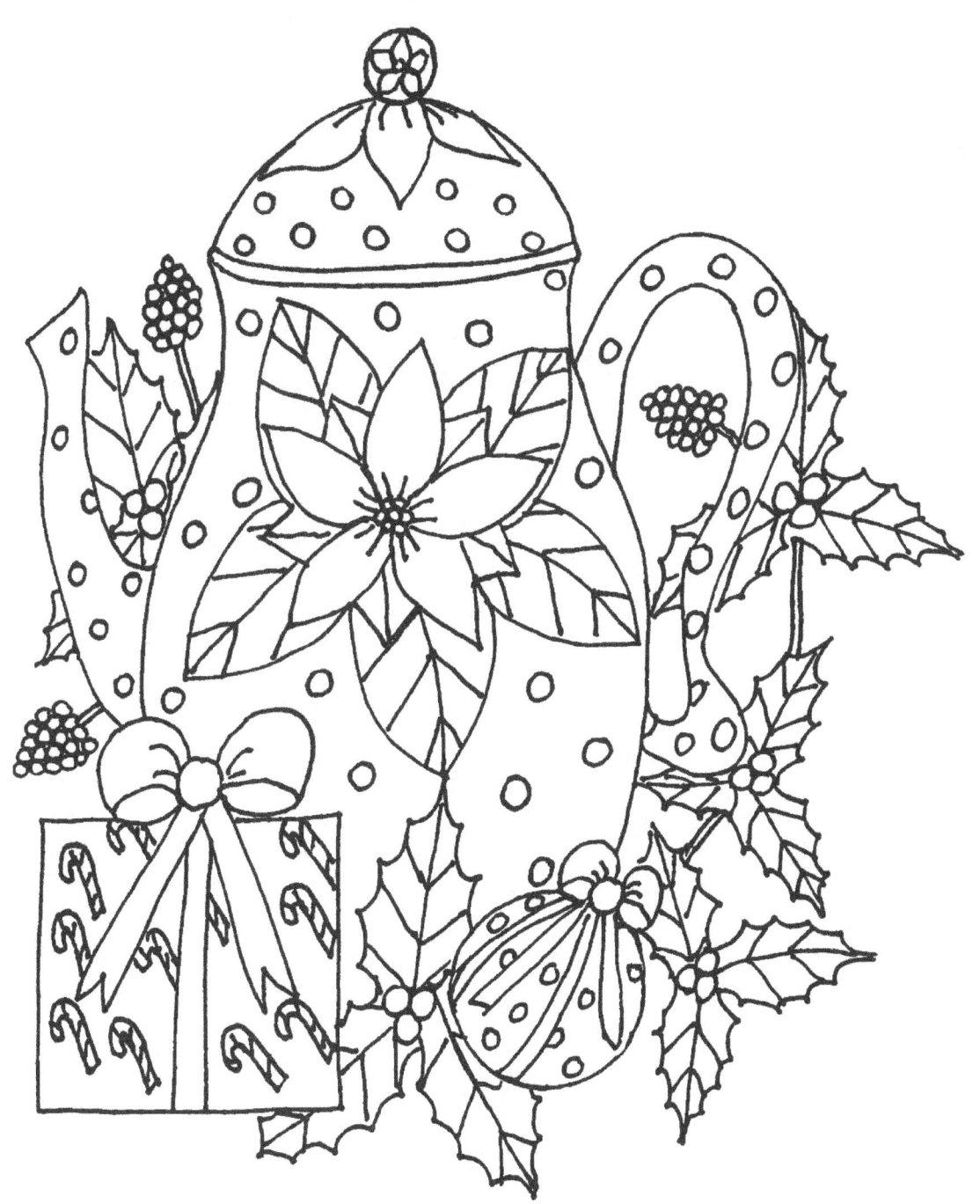

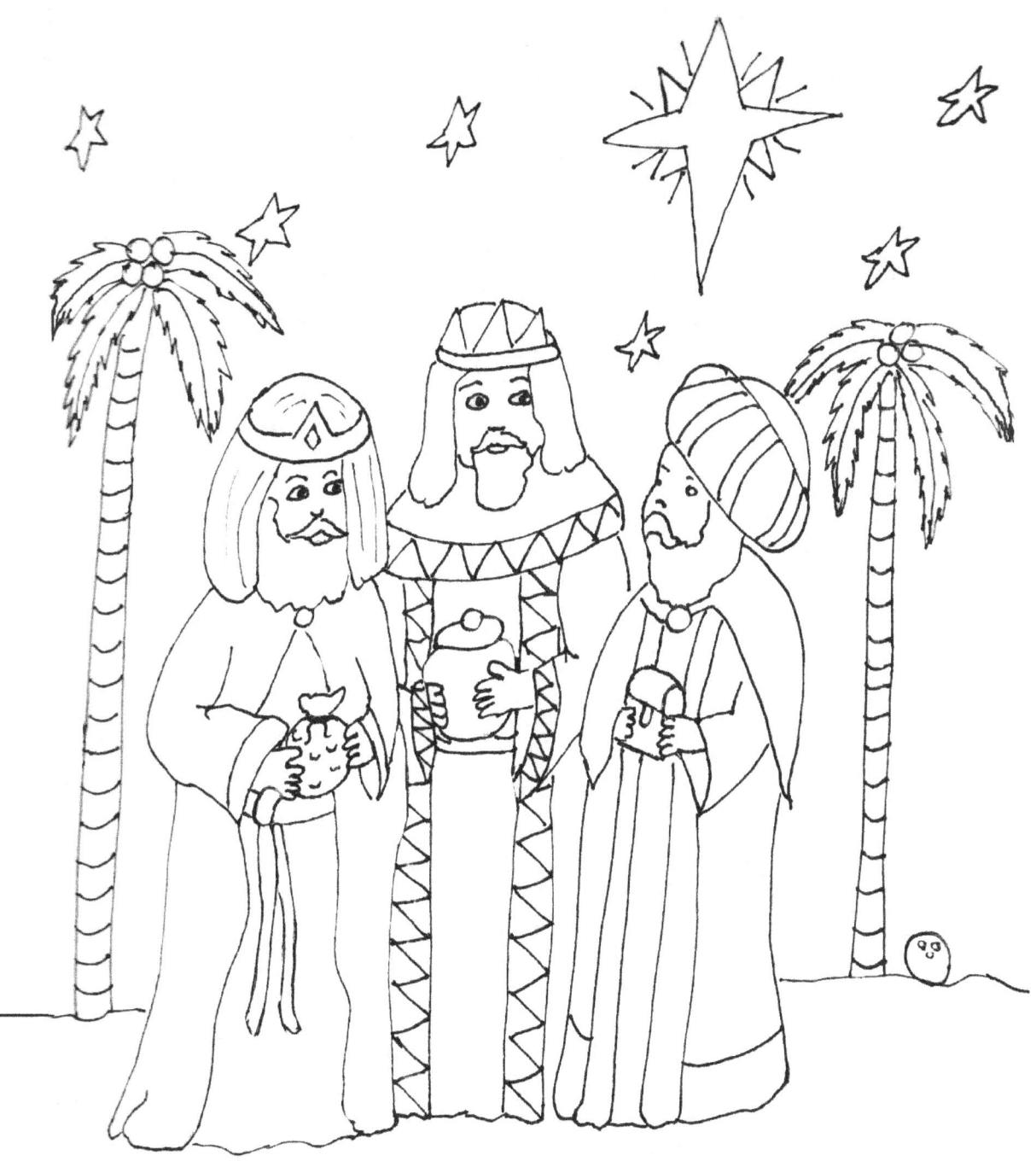

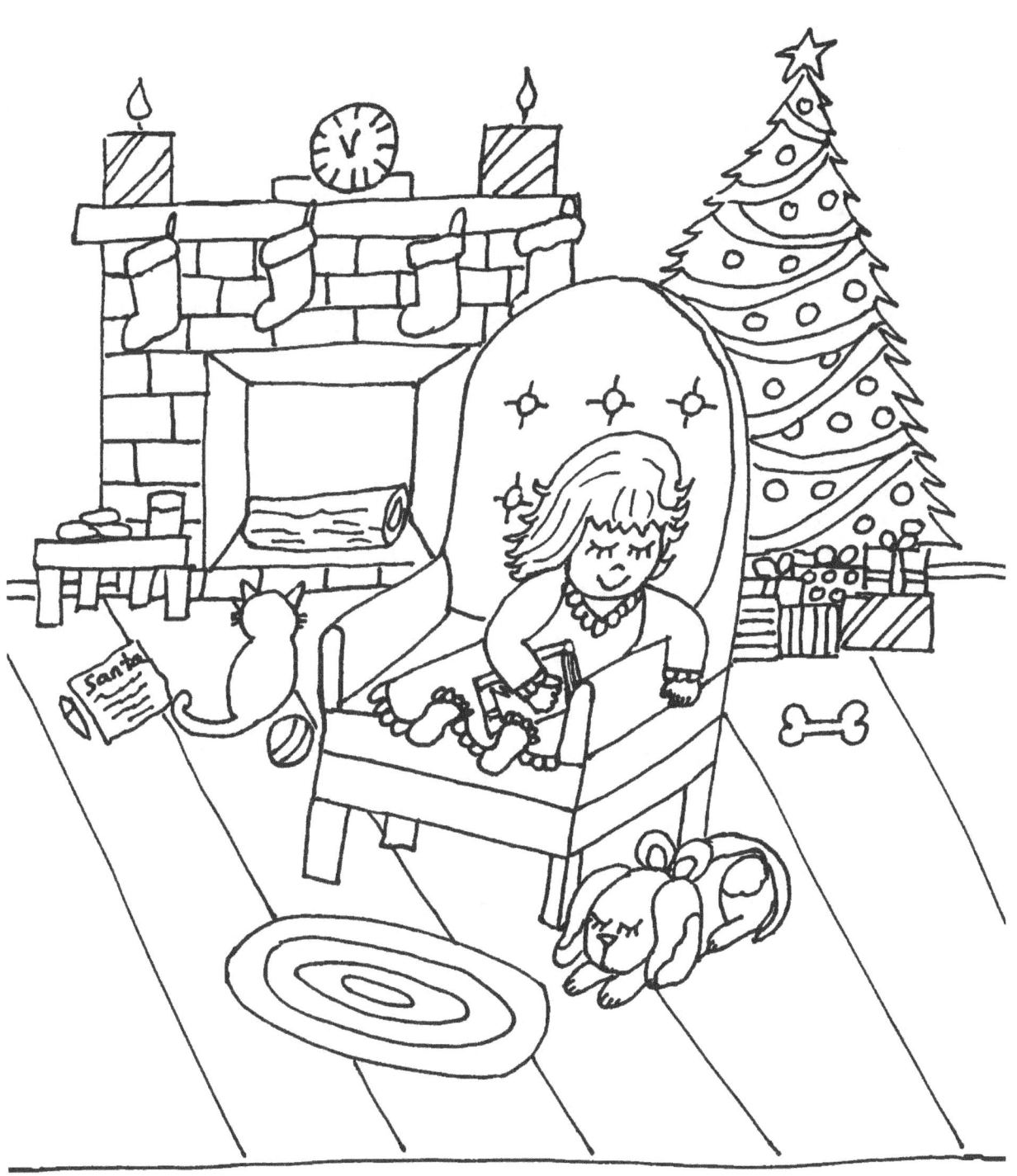

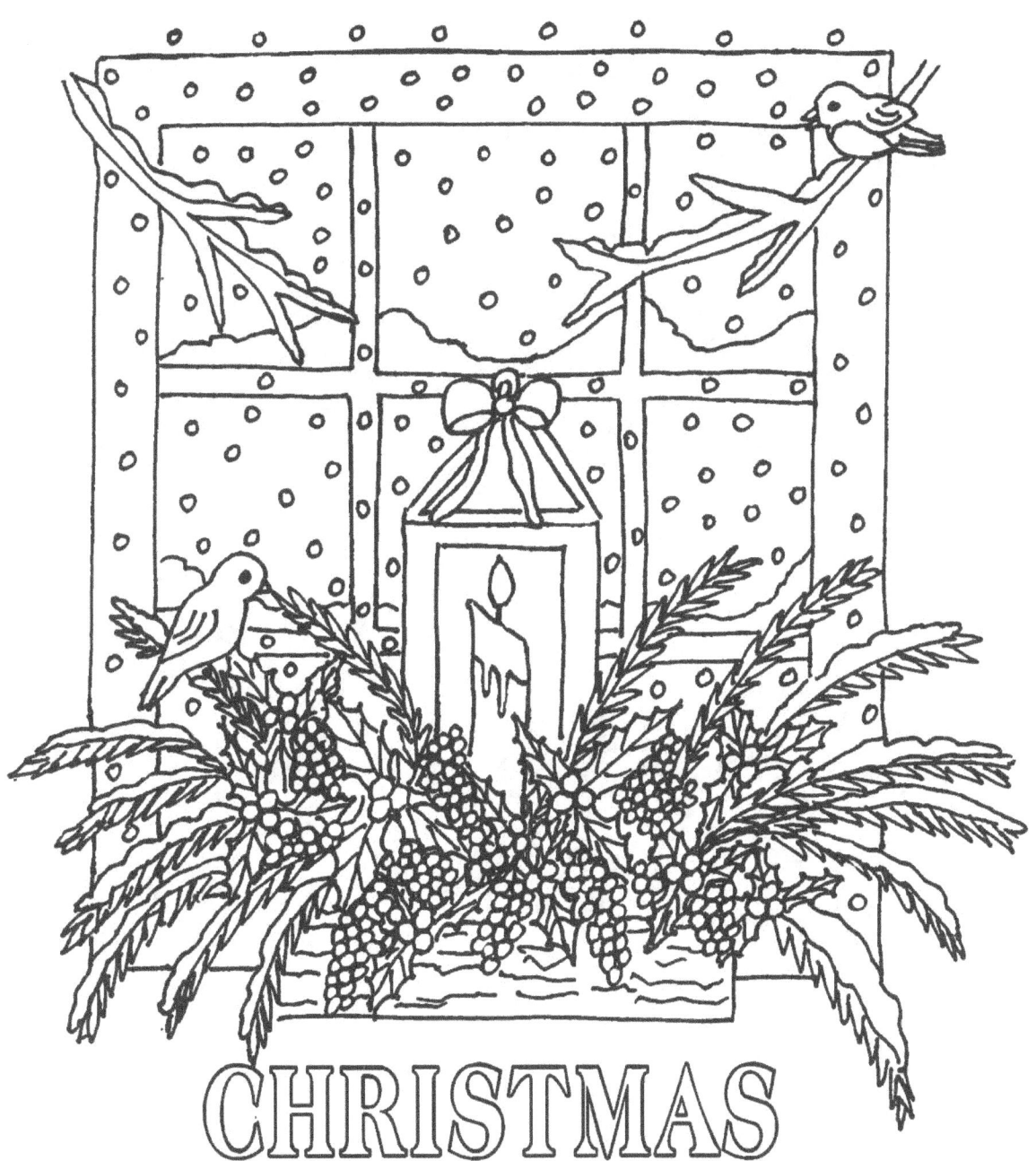

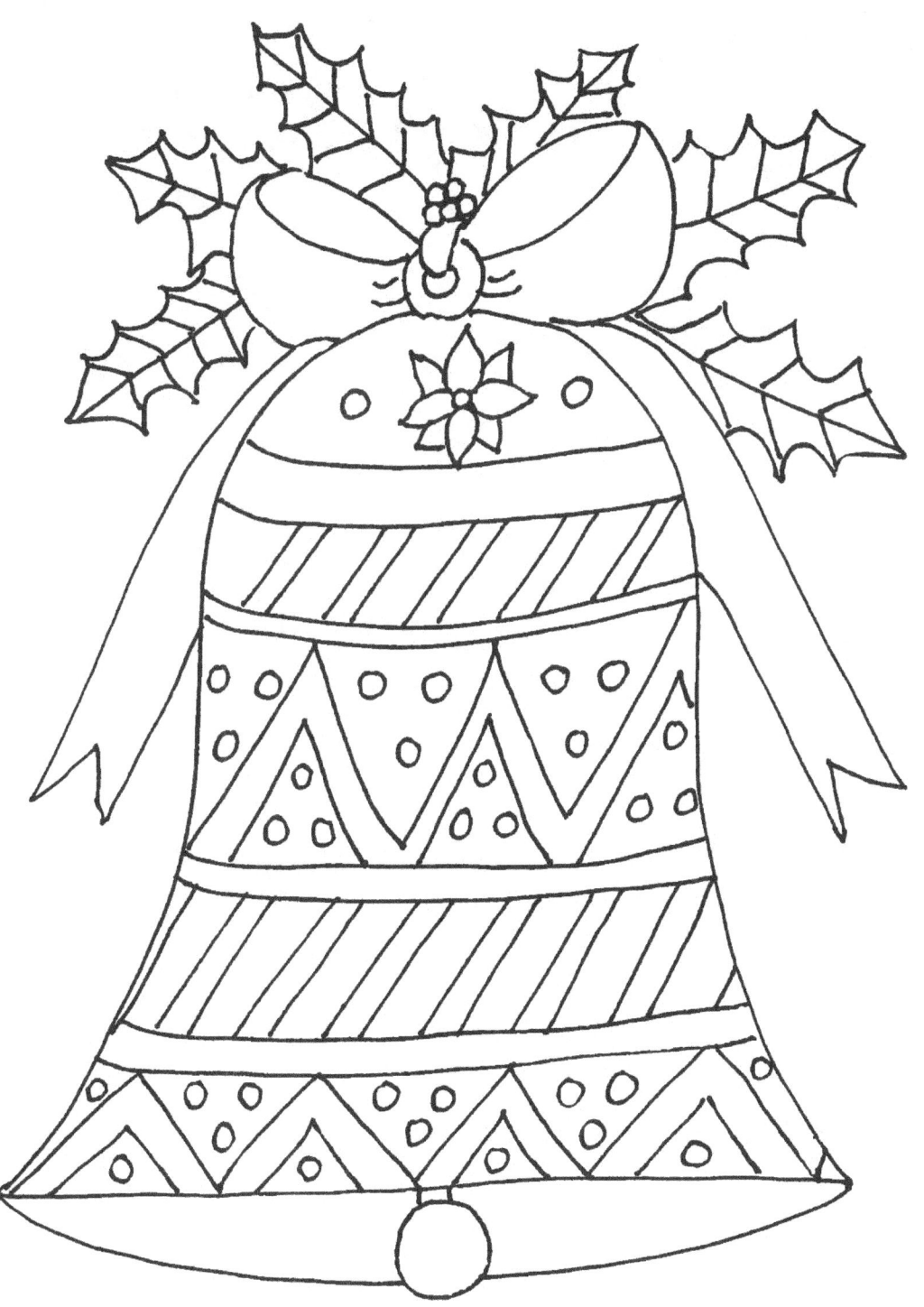

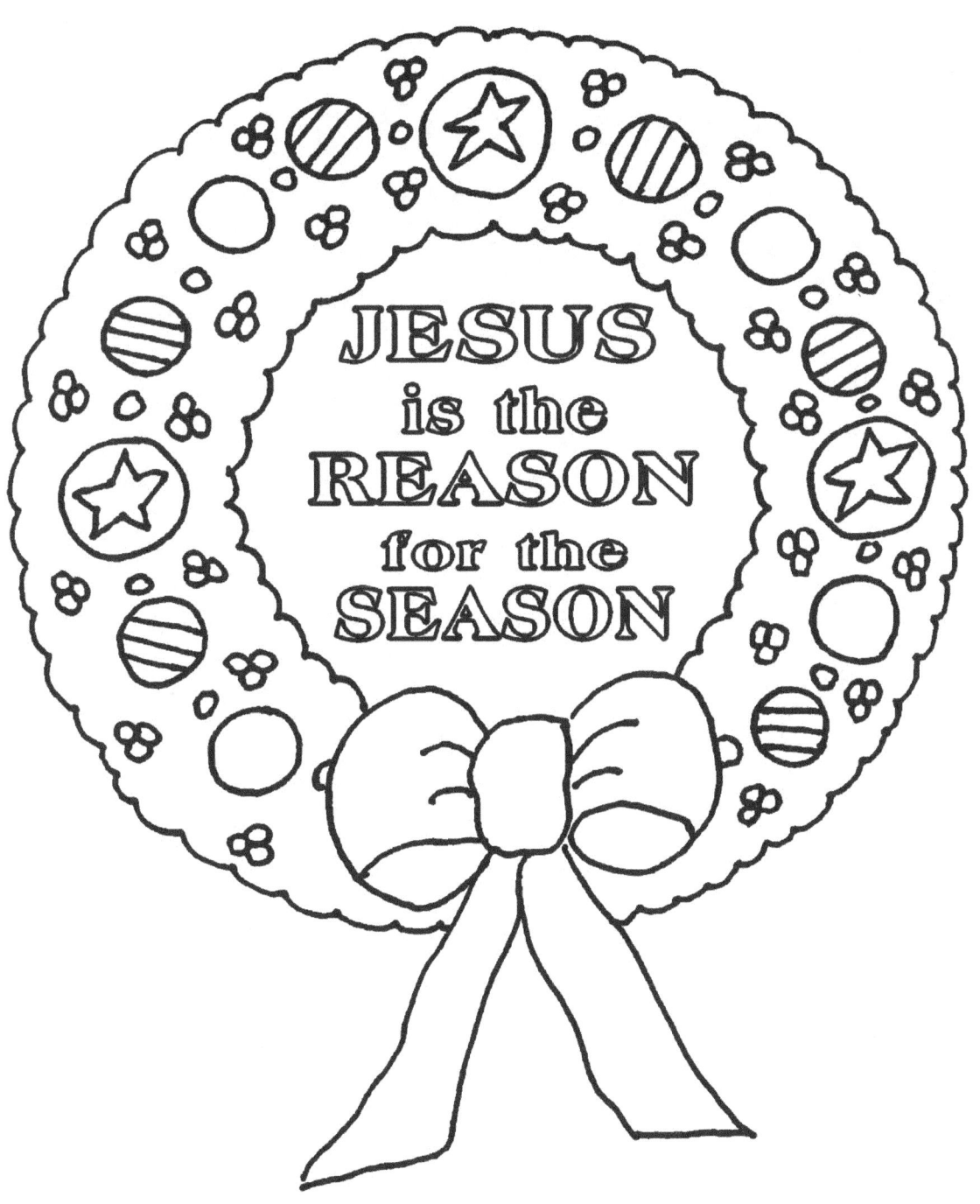

I would like to wish each and every one of you

A Very

MERRY CHRISTMAS

And A

HAPPY NEW YEAR

For more of my coloring books please Visit Amazon

Here is a list of my coloring books

Cute and Whimsical Kids

Birds and Botanicals

Cute and Whimsical Mermaids

Cute and Whimsical Elves

A Collection of Mandalas Book One

A Collection of Mandalas Book Two

A Collection of Mandalas Book Three

Cute Kids and Their Pets

www.ingramcontent.com/pod-product-compliance
Lightning Source LLC
Chambersburg PA
CBHW080001230526
45470CB00008B/2818